The Singing Tree

Arloa Ten Kley

Illustrated by Deborah Smith

ISBN: 978-1-945975-68-4

Published by EA Books Publishing a division of
Living Parables of Central Florida, Inc. a 501c3
EABooksPublishing.com

DEDICATION

To my Mom
Who taught me to love stories,
To love Scripture, and to love God.

"The Lord your God, in your midst,
The Mighty One, will save;
He will rejoice over you with gladness,
He will quiet you with His love,
He will rejoice over you with singing."

Zephaniah 3:17

"Help!"

"This tastes *heavenly*!

You should sell this."

"*Mmm.* Tastes divine."

"Help."

"I'd love to help."

"I can bake."

"I need money for football. *Mmm.* This tastes outta this world!"

"Do you have friends?"

"Yes!"

"It smells heavenly."

"I love this place."

"I love my tree.

My Dad helped me plant it.

Thank you."

"This tree grows like a weed!

My friends and I play near it.

Don't tell them, but I hear the tree sing.

It's my favorite spot."

Sitting, Listening,

Picking,

Washing, Chopping, Baking,

Cleaning,

Selling, *Selling*, **Selling,**

Sitting, Listening.

"My tree has delicious fruit.

I share it with everyone!"

"My buddies – and the birds – love the fruit. When I listen to the sound of the tree, I feel like I can do anything."

"Dear Sir/Madam,

I hope this gets to the right place. I picked up a seedling a few years back, but didn't have time for it. I put it out with the trash. It disappeared. This spring I discovered a tree in the corner of my yard at the bottom of a slope. It must have planted itself. I keep hearing something like music. Does this tree actually sing? "

"Thank you."

ABOUT THE AUTHOR

Arloa Ten Kley has lived in many places around the world, both as a child, and later by choice. She currently resides in Northwest Iowa with her husband. Arloa loves stories, children, animals, and the ways God continually shows up in her life.

The Singing Tree is a delightful story illustrating how one woman found God's Spirit to be present with her. In listening, she found hope, courage, community, -- and hard work! She multiplied her joy by freely giving what she had received, in turn gaining even more connection and spreading hope.

www.ArloaTenKley.com

ABOUT THE ILLUSTRATOR

Deborah's love for art was nurtured at a young age and has developed into an award winning internationally sold artist. Her focus is to honor God through her art. She has taken her love for Christ and her passion for art and incorporated them into her life's work as an illustrator, painter, sculptor, muralist, and teacher.

Prior to her current enthrallment for book illustrating, she had a distinguished and prestigious career as a Disney Artist, Designer, and Art Director. Deborah resides in Orlando, Florida with her husband.

"It truly is a blessing to pursue and share my passion for art. I will never tire of the joy and fulfillment it brings."

www.3-deborah-smith.artistwebsites.com

www.ingramcontent.com/pod-product-compliance
Lightning Source LLC
LaVergne TN
LVHW072121070426
835511LV00002B/48